THE BRIDE REVEALED

REVEALED

An Intimate Look Behind the Wedding Veil

LESLIE BARTON

AND SHERI LEIGH MYERS

**Andrews McMeel
Publishing**

Kansas City

To my husband, Dan, whose love makes everything possible. —Sheri

To my husband, Louis, with whom I'm lucky enough to share deep love.
And to all the brides who changed my life and let me know such love was
possible. —Leslie

05 06 07 08 09 WKT 10 9 8 7 6 5 4 3 2 1

ISBN: 0-7407-5035-6

Library of Congress Control Number: 2004113723

www.lesliebarton.com

BOOK DESIGN BY JUDITH STAGNITTO ABBATE / ABBATE DESIGN

CONTENTS

Introduction

WE HAVE BEEN FRIENDS *since 1991. We first met while working on a film not long after Leslie moved to Southern California. Throughout our friendship we have always talked about creative ideas—something we both have in abundance.*

Many years later, after Leslie's career as a wedding photographer was in full bloom, we decided to do a book with photos drawn from her huge archive of amazing images. From the beginning we knew we wanted to do a book that was real and full of lovely, touching, funny, and sexy moments.

We pored over hundreds of boxes of wedding photos. We pulled each photo that grabbed us: a bride comforting her father in his wheelchair, a young flower girl dancing with her bride, a sexy bride getting laced up in her bustier, a young bride in all of her wedding splendor gazing into the mirror, full of doubt.

We interviewed hundreds of brides, asking them to be as candid as they dared. The stories that unfolded were honest, heartfelt, tender, and funny. (Just so you know, the photos and quotes we have assembled here are emotional, not literal, matches.)

All weddings will have glitches and miracles. Our book is designed to display that full, dazzling spectrum of experience. These brides reveal everything from the anxiety of creating the "perfect" gown (and buttocks to match), to the pleasure of rising above the chaos of the wedding day and discovering exquisite intimacy with their new husbands.

Ultimately, we hope this little book will help everyone to stop looking for perfection and take the mishaps in stride, to "take a slow pill" and appreciate all that is real about a wedding.

That and world peace is all we hope for.

Above all, we are delighted to share our work with you.

CHAPTER ONE
Sea of White

FELT TOO GUILTY TO TELL A SOUL HOW MUCH

I SPENT ON MY GOWN. IT WAS SHEER INDULGENCE. TRUTH IS,

I THINK THE ONLY REASON I WANTED A WEDDING WAS FOR

THE DRESS."

It's not like any other dress. I felt so grown-up and elegant in it. At the same time, it felt like a costume. Even during my wedding, when I saw my reflection, I was startled. 'Who is that?' It's such an important transformation, from the usual jeans and T-shirt to a formal wedding gown. I felt it strengthened the commitment, that what I said on this day would be with me for the rest of my life."

"I was so overwhelmed and tired from my final year of medical school, I hadn't done a thing to prepare for the wedding. My fiancé finally insisted that I go pick out a dress. He made some phone calls and set up an appointment. He loaded me into the car and I slept as he drove to the bridal store. I liked the first dress I tried on, but he wouldn't let me buy it. 'Honey, you have to think about it.'"

I TRIED A BUNCH OF GOWNS ON AND MY SISTERS AND FRIEND WOULD SAY, 'OH, THAT'S NICE...' FINALLY I TRIED ONE ON, AND THEIR JAWS DROPPED. SOMEONE WHISPERED THAT I LOOKED LIKE GRACE KELLY. THAT WAS THE CLINCHER. (YES, I AM GULLIBLE!)"

*"All of my fittings were a joy. I so looked forward
to seeing the gown progress from a piece of muslin,
used for measurements, to a luscious silk and satin
gown that I just wanted to roll around in."*

My veil was magical.

And so simple.

Just one layer of tulle about six feet long. It floated in the wind as I walked down the aisle."

CHAPTER TWO

Torture of Beauty

"*I*T WAS A REVELATION TO SEE WHAT

THE MAKEUP ARTIST DID TO MY FACE. I STILL

LOOKED LIKE ME, ONLY A THOUSAND TIMES BETTER.

AND THAT'S THE WAY IT SHOULD BE, RIGHT?"

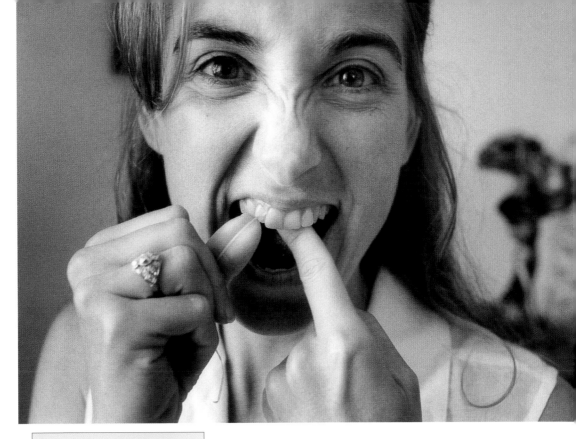

19

LESLIE'S PERSPECTIVE:

I was lucky enough to be flown to an exotic location near Cabo San Lucas to photograph a wedding. This could have been a perfect scenario: beautiful couple, amazing location, gorgeous light. . . .Unfortunately, the bride had a problem with a particular crimp in her bangs. She had that portion of her hair crimped and recrimped for over an hour as I hyperventilated, watching our perfect light fade away.

"I didn't do any dieting or working out.
I figured my fiancé loves me for who I am,
so why try to change for that one day?
It's not worth all the stress."

I AM A BIT SMALL CHESTED BUT WANTED TO HAVE A TINY BIT OF CLEAVAGE. MY DRESS WAS PADDED TO GIVE ME A LIFT. ACTUALLY, IT WAS PADDED TOO MUCH. I LOOK AT MY PICTURES NOW AND REALLY LAUGH. WHAT A PAIR OF KNOCKERS! TOO BAD THEY'RE NOT MINE!"

"I didn't want to get a tan, but since I play a lot of golf, I have very white shoulders and very white feet, in contrast to deep brown arms and legs. There was definitely some urgency to getting rid of the lines, since the dress had a tank top. Unfortunately, it was cold on the days I set aside to tan. I was gardening in the back yard, barefoot, with a scarf around my breasts. Frrreeeeezzzziing!"

$\mathcal{I}$'M GLAD **I** DIDN'T

DECIDE TO DO SOMETHING TOO

OUTRAGEOUS WITH MY HAIR,

because years from now, I won't look back and say, 'What the hell were you thinking?' "

W HEN I WAS FINALLY ALL MADE

UP AND READY FOR PHOTOS, I REMEMBER

LOOKING IN THE MIRROR, THINKING,

'WHO IS THIS PERSON?'"

"*My biggest worry was my deodorant. I had a beautiful sleeveless gown and there would be nothing worse than bridal perspiration. I tested different deodorants for weeks prior to the wedding and then, as expected, I used my standard—Dry Idea. Worked like a charm.*"

CHAPTER THREE

BABES OF HONOR

"I even had my flower girls come to the salon to get their hair done with my bridesmaids. They were such dainty little girls at the beginning of the day, taking special care not to get dirty. Somehow they caught on that the reception is the place to let go, relax, and celebrate. They were running on the grass, falling and laughing and getting grass stains on their dresses, flowers coming out of their hair, hair sticking out all over the place."

"My mother was there with me every step of the way, from early in the morning to the end of the wedding. Her presence added poignancy at just the right moments."

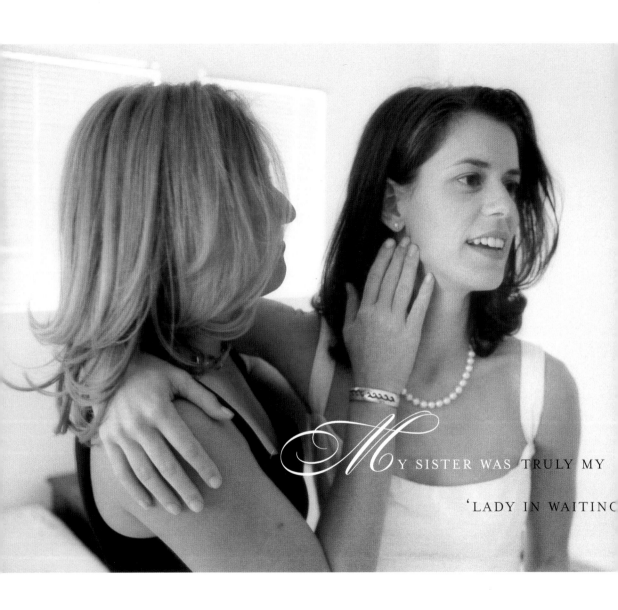

*M*Y SISTER WAS TRULY MY

'LADY IN WAITING

At one particular
wedding, the bride
and her sister, the
maid of honor, were
obviously deeply in love
with each other. The
maid of honor did
everything for the
bride, even before she
knew she needed it.
The experience was
filled with such love
and grace that it
convinced me to have
a second child.

HAT DAY.

She made sure I had everything I
needed. Most importantly, she didn't
take any of my demands personally.
Who could ask for a better sister?
I hope to repay the favor when she
gets married."

"Before the wedding, I thought
I was being pretty cool headed.
I didn't want to be the 'high-
maintenance' bride. Well, after
the ceremony, my bridesmaids and
I went back to the bridal suite to
pin up my train. As they worked on
it, I asked, 'I'm not being too
difficult today, am I?' There was a
long pause, filled with sly smiles.
Then my best friend spoke up. 'You
know bossy Lucy in the Peanuts
comic strip?' They all laughed.
So much for my high definition
of myself!"

THERE REALLY IS SOMETHING WONDERFUL

...ABOUT THE 'GETTING READY' RITUAL.

*You choose your comfort
people to be with you. I wonder
what my grandmothers were
thinking—maybe about their
own lives, watching me grow
up, time passing, who knows.
But having those two women
behind me, looking into the
future with a knowing smile . . .
I knew that along with them,
my mom was there in spirit."*

CHAPTER FOUR

GOD IS KIND

I DO RECALL WHEN I WAS DONE

GETTING READY, LOOKING IN THE MIRROR AND

THINKING THAT GOD WAS VERY KIND TO LET ALL

BRIDES LOOK BEAUTIFUL ON THIS SPECIAL DAY."

I photographed weddings
for nearly twelve years
before I met the man of
my dreams. I was willing
to forgo a wedding. I had
been to enough to satisfy
my wedding urge. It was
my husband who wanted a
wedding. So we had one.
And you know what? It's
true what they say. . . it *is*
one of the best days of
your life. I felt beautiful
and bursting with love,
full of love and fully loved.
If I could put that feeling
into a pill, I'd take it
every day.

*"My fiancé surprised me with a note.
It said, 'I'll see you at 5:15. I'll be the
one waiting at the end of the aisle.' "*

$\mathscr{A}$PPARENTLY, MY DAD HEARD WE WERE ABOUT TO LEAVE AND HE RAN THROUGH THE BUSHES IN THE RAIN TO BE OUT THERE TO KISS HIS DAUGHTER GOOD-BYE. LATER HE TOLD MY MOM THAT HE FELT A SUPERNATURAL SURGE WHEN HE HUGGED ME. THE FEELING WASHED OVER HIM THAT AT LAST I WAS COMPLETELY HAPPY. HE COULD FINALLY RELAX AND LET GO."

"I was nervous as to whether my son would agree to participate. He was only twelve. He knew I was getting married and that I was making all the preparations. Finally, I had to approach him about being part of the ceremony, so I said, 'I would like for you to be my best man, because you are my best man!' He was really pleased and said, 'Yes.'"

"THE FUNNIEST MOMENT WAS WHEN MY GROOM GAVE HIS VOWS AND PROMISED TO STAND BY ME, THROUGH MY EVER-CHANGING HAIR COLORS."

"We went back to our home after the wedding instead of getting a hotel room. It's the best decision we could have made. It was so great waking up the next morning in our own bed. We could go to the fridge for our first glass of OJ as a married couple and curl back up into bed without the worries of a checkout time."

CHAPTER FIVE

WHAT THE HELL

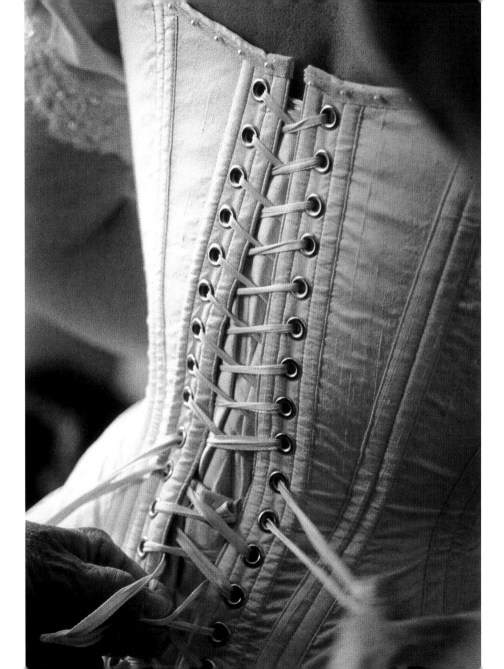

$\mathscr{M}$Y CORSET WAS PULLED SO TIGHT I COULDN'T

GET A DEEP BREATH THE WHOLE DAY WITHOUT WORRYING I MIGHT

SPLIT A SEAM! HONEST TO GOD, I THOUGHT THE COLOR PHOTOS

MIGHT SHOW ME A PALE SHADE OF BLUE FROM LACK OF OXYGEN."

I was making myself crazy! I kept wondering what I'd do if my groom didn't show up. We were getting married on an island and I was afraid that he would, literally, miss the boat. Also, I was four months pregnant, nobody knew, and I was worried that everyone would talk about how fat I looked."

"My husband said he wouldn't marry me if I didn't quit smoking, so I chose to quit right before the ceremony."

OUR WEDDING NIGHT

CONSISTED OF MY HUSBAND RUBBING

NEOSPORIN ON MY BOTTOM.

I had two thousand pinpricks. My bustle had broken and we had used stickpins to keep it in place. I didn't even know I was getting stuck, I was on such an adrenaline rush all day. I sure could feel it later. I couldn't sit, lie down, or get into the Jacuzzi. Not exactly how we had planned it!"

"*My hairdresser bailed at the last minute. Refused to come and do my hair at 6:30 A.M. Her replacement spent the entire time complaining that I wasn't paying her enough. What a sweet way to start my wedding day! I waited until she was finished, shoved the cash in her hand, and said, 'Now you can go back to bed.'*"

"During the ceremony, I could hear crackling and crunching sounds from the front row. My sister-in-law had given my nephews bags of chips to snack on. The noise drove me nuts. I had to fight the urge to stop the ceremony and scream at them to keep quiet."

LESLIE'S PERSPECTIVE:

In my very early days, I worked for a mom and pop studio in a small town near Madison, Wisconsin. Every Saturday, they would give me a camera, film, and a set of names and directions to the wedding. One such wedding was held in a small church in rural Wisconsin. The bride looked about twelve and weighed sixty-five pounds. After the ceremony, the women went down to the basement for the reception and the men went outside to smoke and cuss and spit.

I HAD A VERY WEIRD FEELING WHEN I REALIZED THAT, FOR BETTER OR WORSE, I WAS COMMITTING TO THIS ONE PERSON FOR THE REST OF MY LIFE!"

CHAPTER SIX

This is It

*B*EFORE THEY CALLED ME TO GO DOWN,

I REMEMBER THINKING, 'EVERYTHING IS GOING

TO BE DIFFERENT FROM THIS DAY ON.

"Many people thought they were being invited to my wedding, but they were really coming to my coronation."

Everything is changing, but for the better.' I was also a little scared, but I told myself, 'Okay, there's no going back. They're all downstairs waiting. This is it!' "

*A*S MY DAD WALKED THROUGH

THE DOOR OF THE BRIDAL COTTAGE,

HE SAW ME, FELL AGAINST THE DOOR FRAME,

AND BURST INTO TEARS.

It took him about ten minutes to collect himself. It is a moment I will never forget as long as I live. All I could think was, 'How lucky I am to have a father who loves me so much!' Needless to say, I was crying, too."

"Before I walked down the aisle I saw my son, and I noticed a tear running down his cheek. I had never seen him so vulnerable. We made eye contact, and in a flash I assured him that he wasn't losing me, that our lives would be richer than before. He assured me that he was willing to share me. We both cried, sad to let go of our life together and joyful to welcome our new life and our new family."

"My adorable little nephew walked out with the ring before me, so he kind of broke the ice. I was glad someone could have the attention. Maybe I could sneak in behind him!"

LESLIE'S
PERSPECTIVE:

My assistant and I used to observe the bride and groom at weddings to see if they had truly surrendered themselves to each other. Surrendered in a good way, in that they were totally committed, open, and real with each other. Sometimes one had surrendered and not the other. On occasion, both of them had surrendered. You could tell by the way they touched that they were in the full, warm gush of love.

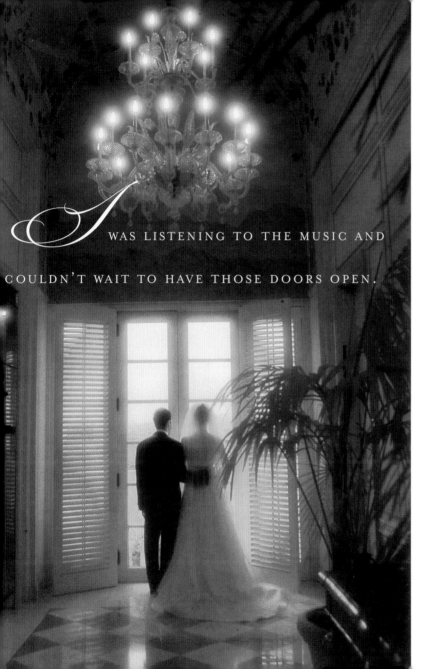

I WAS LISTENING TO THE MUSIC AND COULDN'T WAIT TO HAVE THOSE DOORS OPEN.

Every person I loved and who loved me was going to witness my vows to my true love. I couldn't wait for them to see how incredibly happy I was."

59

CHAPTER SEVEN

EXTRA CREDIT

A TRIED TO DO THE SEXY UNDERWEAR THING,

but my real issue was fitting into the dress. With both a push-up bra and a body shaper, I was wrapped up tighter than a bull's ass at fly time. I tell you, I felt like a knockwurst in that thing. Because I had that vice grip on, I didn't want my husband to undress me. I ended up changing in the bathroom and made my entrance in my nightgown. Honestly, we were so blown away about being married and so tired we could have passed on the sex. But we didn't want being tired to keep us from expressing this monumental thing. He was so sweet and romantic, staring into my eyes and holding my face, calling me his wife and whispering how lucky he was to have me. I felt like I was in a dream."

I felt very sexy in my wedding gown, which was form-fitting satin. My 'something blue' was a G-string from Trashy Lingerie. (It was the only thing I had on under the dress.) Trashy's G-string feels like you have nothing on at all."

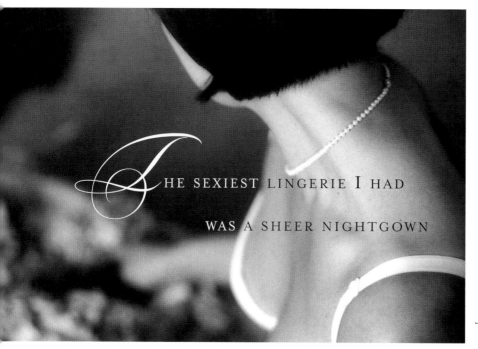

$\mathcal{T}$HE SEXIEST LINGERIE I HAD

WAS A SHEER NIGHTGOWN

and slippers that my mom gave me. Her note said, 'You don't have to have sex on your wedding night, but if you do, you get extra credit.' Without divulging any details, I'll just say that we made full use of that outfit, including the high-heeled slippers."

"As I was slipping on my garter, I thought of him and how he'd be taking it off later. It was 3 A.M. when we returned to our room from the midnight cruise. My husband slowly undressed me from top to bottom whispering, 'I can't believe you're mine.' We snuggled and fell blissfully asleep."

LESLIE'S
PERSPECTIVE:

In my early days, I used to
shoot weddings on a boat
that would cruise around
the harbor in Los Angeles.
We were a captive audience,
so no one missed the show.
Once, after the cake was
cut, the bride and her
drop-dead gorgeous
bridesmaid reappeared
quite scantily clad to do a
lap dance on the groom,
smothering him in their
hair and breasts. It was a
surprise for the groom
(and everyone else).

*"With the help of a close friend, we were upgraded
to the presidential suite at a swanky hotel on the
beach. My God, it was bigger than my house! Four
TVs, a washer-dryer, three kitchens . . . I took off
all my clothes and just ran around the place. Of
course we did it—in every room! Come on, you
have to have sex in the presidential suite!"*

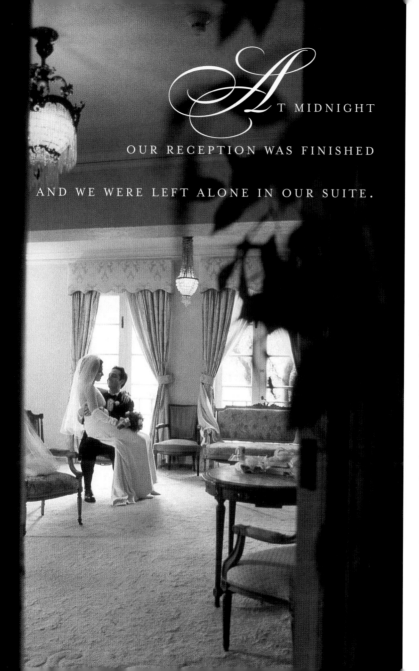

$\mathcal{A}$ T MIDNIGHT

OUR RECEPTION WAS FINISHED

AND WE WERE LEFT ALONE IN OUR SUITE.

The last forty-eight hours had been so full of commotion and now with the close of a door, it was dead quiet. My husband gave me a hug and I felt huge waves of emotion wash over me—the joy of being married, relief that the wedding went smoothly, and sadness that it was over. My husband held me close as I cried. It was the most intimate moment of the entire event."

WE VOWED THAT NO MATTER WHAT, WE WERE GOING TO MAKE LOVE ON OUR WEDDING NIGHT.

We bopped around, having fun until the wee hours. When we finally got back to our suite, we were exhausted. As I was taking off my beautiful dress, thinking only of passing out in bed, my husband said, 'Leave the veil on.' Yahoo!"

"We dated for seven years. All summer before the wedding, he wanted to start trying to get pregnant. I said, 'No,' because I didn't know how I'd feel the first trimester and I wanted to look my best. On our wedding night, I gave him a huge bottle of prenatal vitamins and took some on the spot. As far as we've been able to calculate, our first child was conceived that night."

CHAPTER EIGHT

TAKE A SLOW PILL

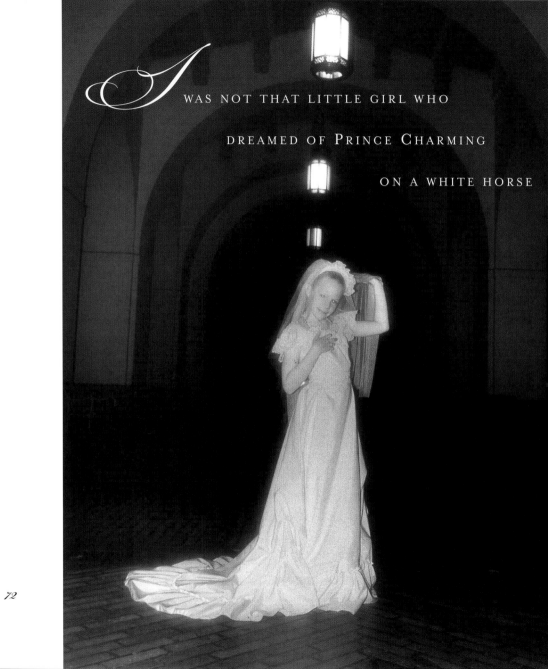

I WAS NOT THAT LITTLE GIRL WHO

DREAMED OF PRINCE CHARMING

ON A WHITE HORSE

and a $200,000
wedding day with doves,
a horse-drawn carriage,
and all that jazz. Many
of my girlfriends had
their locations picked out
years before there was a
potential mate in the
picture. I didn't start
envisioning the day until
I met my husband, so
I didn't have all those
little girl expectations to
fulfill."

"Make sure you understand
the differences between your
religion and your fiancé's. It
can definitely affect how you
plan your wedding!"

"My advice to brides is to spend the money on your photographer. Get the best you can. How many times are you going to pull your wedding gown out of storage? But your photos will always be there. So they'd better be good!"

LESLIE'S
PERSPECTIVE:

My advice from a photographer's point of view: Have your ceremony during the late afternoon sunlight. (We photographers call it the "magic hour.") Then everything that follows will bask in the beautiful evening glow. Light makes all the difference. My best advice: Above all, be joyous!

"One thing to remember: Include everybody. It's much better to include someone than to hurt their feelings later on, especially family."

MY FEET GOT TIRED BY II P.M.,

SO I SWITCHED TO MY SNEAKERS."

"We were worried that one of my brothers, who's an alcoholic, would show up at the wedding drunk. My priest and therapist both advised us to assign two people to watch over him that day. Fortunately, he was fine, but we were prepared."

𝒪UR PRIEST SAID, 'YOU TWO ARE ALREADY MARRIED.

Your souls are already connected. The wedding is for the families, the two tribes coming together to celebrate the dance.'"

*"Your honeymoon
is for long walks
and room service.
Forget about
Disneyland!"*

$\mathscr{A}$CKNOWLEDGMENTS

WE HOLD *a deep sense of gratitude for the brides who so generously shared their stories and allowed us to show their photographs. They not only made this book possible but also made the making of the book a joy. It is a privilege to know such fine women.*

A sincere and heartfelt thank-you to Robert Cavalli of Still Moving Pictures in Los Angeles. His enthusiasm and sensitivity in printing the photographs added immeasurably to our book.

Thank you to Amber Medley for not only being a great assistant but also for her expertise and hard work with the digital aspects of producing this book.

Thank you to Jennifer London, another wonderful assistant of years ago, who took the photograph on page 75 at Leslie's wedding.

Our deep appreciation to Polly Blair at Andrews McMeel Publishing who has been a joy to work with. Her excitement for the material was contagious.

Creating a book is a long and complex project. There have been so many others who have generously offered their support and feedback. We are filled with gratitude.